CREATE YOUR OWN
GREETING CARDS
& GIFT WRAP
WITH *Priscilla Hauser*

CREATE YOUR OWN

GREETING CARDS
& GIFT WRAP

WITH *Priscilla Hauser*

Priscilla Wait Hauser

NORTH LIGHT BOOKS

Cincinnati, Ohio

Disclaimer: The information in this book is presented in good faith, but no warranty is given, nor results guaranteed, nor is freedom from any patent to be inferred. Since we have no control over physical conditions surrounding the application of information herein contained, Priscilla Hauser and North Light Books disclaim any liability for untoward results.

Warning: Due to the components used in this craft, children under eight years of age should not have access to the components used, or be allowed to play with the finished craft projects, without adult supervision. Components or projects could cause serious or fatal injury.

Important: Please be sure to thoroughly read the instructions for all products used to complete projects in this book, paying particular attention to all cautions and warnings shown for each product to ensure its proper and safe use.

Create Your Own Greeting Cards and Gift Wrap With Priscilla Hauser. Copyright © 1994 by Priscilla S. Hauser. Printed and bound in Hong Kong. All rights reserved. No part of this book may be reproduced in any form or by any electronic or mechanical means including information storage and retrieval systems without permission in writing from the publisher, except by a reviewer, who may quote brief passages in a review. Published by North Light Books, an imprint of F&W Publications, Inc., 1507 Dana Avenue, Cincinnati, Ohio 45207. 1-800-289-0963. First edition.

This hardcover edition of *Create Your Own Greeting Cards and Gift Wrap With Priscilla Hauser* features a "self-jacket" that eliminates the need for a separate dust jacket. It provides sturdy protection for your book while it saves paper, trees and energy.

98 97 96 95 94   5 4 3 2 1

Library of Congress Cataloging-in-Publication Data

Hauser, Priscilla.
   Create your own greeting cards and gift wrap with Priscilla Hauser / by Priscilla Wait Hauser.
       p.   cm.
   Includes index.
   ISBN 0-89134-519-1
   1. Greeting cards. 2. Gift wraps. I. Title.
TT872.H38   1994
745.54 — dc20   94-3100
                                                              CIP

Edited by Jenny Pfalzgraf
Cover and interior design by Brian Roeth

METRIC CONVERSION CHART		
TO CONVERT	**TO**	**MULTIPLY BY**
Inches	Centimeters	2.54
Centimeters	Inches	0.4
Feet	Centimeters	30.5
Centimeters	Feet	0.03
Yards	Meters	0.9
Meters	Yards	1.1
Sq. Inches	Sq. Centimeters	6.45
Sq. Centimeters	Sq. Inches	0.16
Sq. Feet	Sq. Meters	0.09
Sq. Meters	Sq. Feet	10.8
Sq. Yards	Sq. Meters	0.8
Sq. Meters	Sq. Yards	1.2
Pounds	Kilograms	0.45
Kilograms	Pounds	2.2
Ounces	Grams	28.4
Grams	Ounces	0.04

About the Author

Priscilla Hauser has taught decorative painting and crafts for over thirty years, drawing the enthusiasm of thousands of students around the world. She has authored numerous instructional books, appeared in four television series and is the founder of the National Society of Tole and Decorative Painters, an organization of over 34,000 members. Her work appears regularly in *Decorative Artist's Workbook* and numerous other craft publications.

Dedication

To Logan Leslie Langworthy Mitchell

Acknowledgments

Thanks to all who helped make this book possible:
- Carolyn Curry
- Kathy Meeker
- Judy Kimball
- Mona Kochendorfer
- Evelyn Carter
- Janet Stewart
- Malinda Johnston
- Mary Ellen Campbell
- Pat Tanguay
- Charlene Garri
- Jane Jenkins

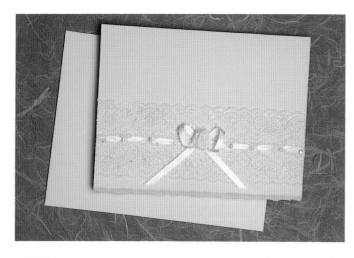

Table of Contents

Introduction

A greeting card is special and personal. It is a thought or wish that you have chosen to send to someone you care about.

Beautiful greeting cards and gift sets can be purchased, but if you take a little time, you can make your own. Those specially created by hand are often much more meaningful to the recipient. The fact that you have spent time and energy to create a card for someone means more than any sentiment you can buy commercially.

What's more, creating your own cards and gift wrap is loads of fun and is not expensive. Often, household items can be used. Remnant items can be recycled to produce beautiful, one-of-a-kind cards. Even store-bought craft supplies are reasonably priced. Card making is a wonderful hobby for people of all ages.

This book will provide you with a wealth of ideas. You'll find cards and gift sets for almost every occasion. As you look through the chapters, you'll discover some magnificent crafting techniques. Go through a few of the projects, step-by-step and learn some new skills. Soon, your imagination will be sparked and you'll be inventing new designs and new projects on your own. Use this book as an idea source to fuel your own creative impulses. It is my hope you'll find the projects in this book to be a real inspiration.

Think of the special ones you'd like to remember with handcrafted cards and begin to plan. You'll quickly discover how easy and inexpensive it is—and how good it makes you feel creating and giving these special mementos.

Chapter One

BASIC INFORMATION

Before you get started on the projects in this book, take a few moments to read through this chapter covering the basics. It's important to understand the unique qualities of the tools and materials you're working with—and perhaps more important to know where to look for ideas.

Once you know your materials, you'll be ready to improvise on the projects shown in this book and make them truly your own. Furthermore, once you find your own unique sources for ideas, your creativity will take on a life of its own and expand far beyond the pages of this book. Have a great time!

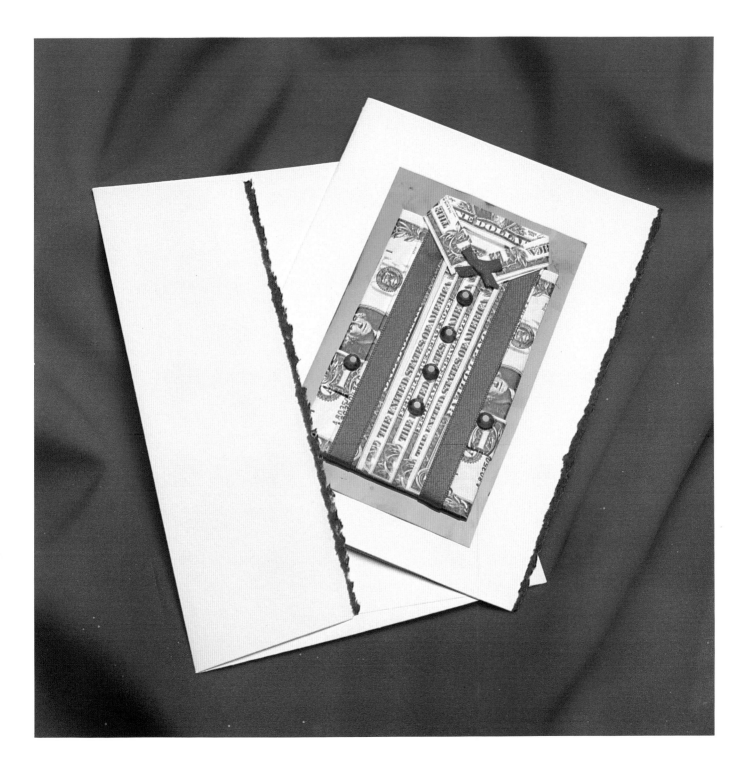

Finding Ideas

Perhaps the most exciting, yet most challenging aspect to making your own cards and gift creations is coming up with new and unique ideas. It's important to find idea "sources" to get your creative juices flowing.

Every person has his or her own unique ways of looking for new ideas, and you will find yours. I keep an "idea file" at home. It is simply a cedar chest that I put things in, such as magazine and newspaper clippings, fabric and wallpaper swatches, paint swatches, poems, quotes, letters, bits of lace, and an assortment of old jewelry, beads, buttons and charms. I often open this box of treasures when I'm stumped and need inspiration. It's almost like having a multi-faceted diary.

I also keep a "special occasion reference" — a notebook with the dates of birthdays, anniversaries, graduations, holidays and other special occasions. I include names and addresses of people I want to remember with cards. I try to update the notebook every month so that I can plan my time and be sure not to forget any special people in my life.

Another great way to spark ideas is simply to get out in the world and see what materials are available for craft purposes. Flea markets are great places to find unusual materials, scraps, and odds and ends. Also art, craft and fabric stores, flower shops, and even hardware stores, are great places to find ideas.

Most important, talk about your ideas with friends and family. They may have some valuable suggestions!

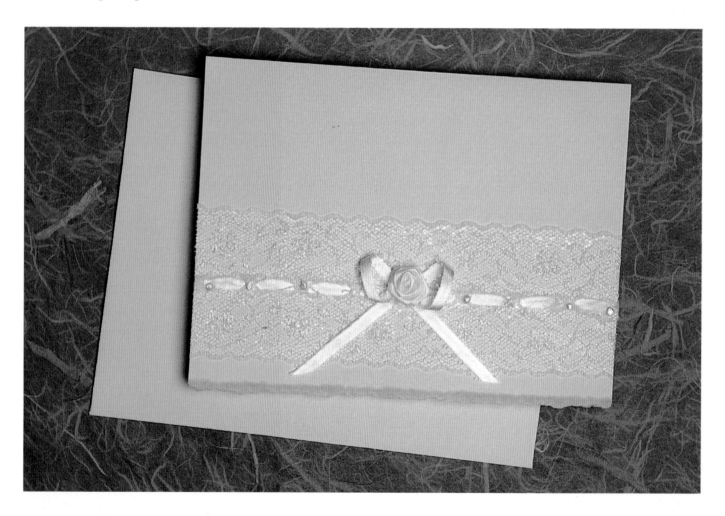

Materials

This book covers a multitude of techniques in a wide variety of media. It's important to understand how different materials behave and when to use them. Below, you'll find a basic overview of the major materials you'll be using for the projects in this book.

Paper

Many of the cards in this book were created from scratch, but some are simply plain cards that have been embellished in a variety of ways. Card stock can be purchased at most any art, craft or stationery store. Pre-folded cards and envelopes come in a variety of shapes, sizes, colors and weights. Some even come with deckled edges, die cuts and other unique attributes.

If you choose to cut and fold your own cards, experiment with different types of paper. I often use construction paper, Canson paper, watercolor paper or plain writing paper. Remember to use a heavier paper stock or even cardboard if you plan to attach heavy items to your card.

When printing wrapping paper, try using butcher paper, newsprint, brown grocery paper, newspaper (comics sections too), or any assortment of fine papers (such as rice or tissue paper) available on the market.

Glue

Almost all of the projects in this book involve glue in some form or another. Before gluing any items, consider the nature of the objects you are working with and the results you hope to achieve. Choose your glue accordingly. Contrary to popular belief, all glues are not the same:

Tacky glue
A basic, white, all-purpose glue. It dries clear and flexible. Can be used for most paper and fabric crafts.

Designer's glue
A heavy, durable white glue used for heavy-duty gluing. Use this type of glue to attach heavy objects (such as charms or jewelry) to cardboard or heavy card stock.

Glue guns
These tools must be plugged into electrical outlets. Glue guns were once dangerously hot, but now low-temp guns are available on the market. Clear glue sticks are inserted into the back of the gun. The glue melts and shoots out the front. This type of glue is clear and dries extremely quickly. It works best for attaching lightweight materials (such as bits of lace or tiny pearls) in small spots. Because it dries almost immediately, this glue is not spreadable.

Sizing
An adhesive designed specifically for gold and silver leafing. It has an extremely thin consistency—much like nail polish.

Acrylic spray mount
Aerosol spray used to cover large, flat surfaces (for example, if you wish to fuse two pieces of paper together).

Paint

Like glue, paint is used in almost every project in this book. Before using any old paint, think about the unique qualities of different types of paint and the effects you hope to achieve.

Watercolor
Obviously, a water-based paint. Best for creating translucent effects, or very slight hints of color. Dries quickly.

Acrylic
Perhaps the most versatile paint. It can be thinned down to wash consistency (much like watercolor) or can be used thicker for bright, opaque effects. This water-based paint dries quickly.

Oil
Definitely the messiest and most hazardous paint. Oils take the longest to dry. Nevertheless, certain effects (such as marbleizing paper) can only be achieved with oils. Oils can also be used on top of water-soluble inks without causing the ink to run.

Dimensional paint
Water-based craft paints that come in small squeeze bottles in a wide variety of colors. They can be used for detail work (applied directly from the bottle) or can be squeezed out onto a palette and used like other paints. As the name indicates, dimensional paints can maintain a thick "puffy" consistency when dry. They are great for outlining.

Odds and ends

In reading through the projects in this book, you'll find that almost all the cards contain odds and ends of a sort: beads, buttons, charms, fabric swatches, paper scraps, bits of lace, dried flowers, ribbons—you name it, there's a use for it. After reading about some of these projects, you may think twice before throwing anything away!

Tools

There are certain tools I always like to have by my side, for which I always seem to find some use:

Stylus

A multipurpose tool that can be used for stirring, scoring, embossing, holding delicate items in place, or even applying glue or paint to tight spots.

Utility knife

Often more practical than scissors, this versatile tool can be used to cut windows, straight edges and tiny shapes for which scissors are too clumsy. Be sure to keep your blade sharp at all times.

Sponges

I love sponges and use them in many different ways: painting, printing, mopping and cleaning up.

Brushes

For the most part, I use synthetic brushes whenever I paint. I keep a variety of flats, rounds, liners and other assorted styles for specific purposes. Experiment with different types of brushes and decide which ones you like best. Be sure to keep oil brushes separate from those used for water-based paints.

Basic Techniques

Before you get started on projects, here are some basic techniques that will be used repeatedly in this book. They are simple touches that add pizzazz or elegance to any card.

Flyspecking

Flyspecking creates a soft, pebbly effect that is pleasing to the eye. Often, it is the perfect finishing touch for a classy card. All you need is a toothbrush, some heavy card stock, any kind of paint and a steady hand.

Squeeze the paint colors of your choice onto a palette and thin to wash consistency. If you're working with watercolor or acrylic, thin with water. Oils, on the other hand, must be thinned with turpentine. Load a toothbrush with paint and hold it over your paper or card surface. Pull your thumb gently over the bristles to speckle the paint onto the surface. If you desire, rinse the brush and repeat the process with a different color.

Deckled edge

One of the simplest, quickest, most effective ways to dress up a plain-looking card is to add a deckled edge. A deckled edge is a torn or frayed piece of paper which forms the edge of a card.

You can buy ready-made cards and stationery with a deckled edge, but it is fun and easy to do it yourself. Plus, if you tear the edge yourself, you can achieve more variety. Experiment with different types of paper. Each will tear a bit differently.

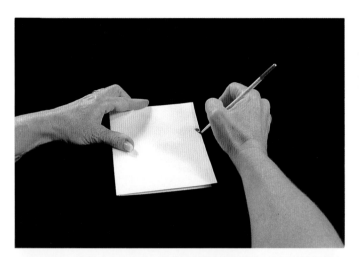

1 Choose the paper you wish to use (I used 140-lb. watercolor paper here) and fold your card. Dampen the edge of the card, but don't soak it. The paper may warp if it gets too wet.

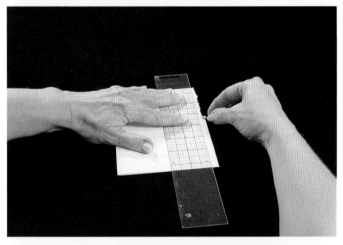

2 Place a ruler approximately ¼ inch in from the edge. Carefully tear the edge, pulling toward yourself.

3 Once the edge is dry, you may wish to dress it up with a light wash of watercolor. Here, I used a tiny bit of brown madder mixed with alizarin crimson. The color choice is up to you.

Window cards

To create a three-dimensional effect, consider making a window card. Windows can be filled with everything from photographs to dried flowers, to special notes. Be sure to use a durable paper stock (such as watercolor paper) for window cards so that the paper won't tear.

1 First cut out the shape for your window with scrap paper. You'll use this shape as a pattern. Here, I folded my paper in quarters and cut an arc to get a perfect oval pattern.

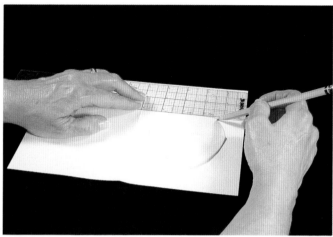

2 Trace the pattern onto your card.

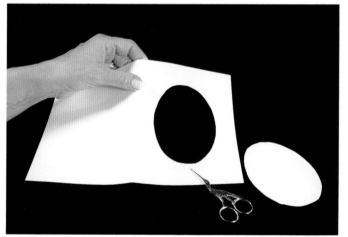

3 Cut out the shape with scissors or a utility knife. Make sure you only cut through one side of the card.

4 Decorate the window as you wish. Here I added sticker pansies for a feminine springtime card.

Chapter Two

COLLAGE

Collage is perhaps the easiest and most inexpensive route to making fabulous cards. A potpourri of ordinary household objects and craft supplies can become wonderful gifts in no time. Before making a trip to the store, take a look around your own home for card-worthy items. I like to use scraps of paper, used wrapping paper, wallpaper swatches, buttons, beads, magazine clippings, fabric remnants—you name it. With a little imagination, the most ordinary items can be transformed into the perfect gift to brighten someone's day.

Of course, a variety of materials and adorable accessories can be purchased at art, fabric and craft stores as well. You'll find an assortment of wood cutouts, charms, toys and other baubles that are perfect for cards and gift sets. Sometimes just looking through the shelves will spur all kinds of ideas.

This chapter will explore a wide variety of projects in numerous styles. Most of the card creations are simply a matter of arranging objects and gluing them in place. You may want to use a glue gun (with clear glue sticks) when working with delicate, lightweight materials such as lace or tiny beads. Heavier materials, such as cardboard and heavy charms, will require a sturdier white glue.

Try some of these projects out for yourself, or simply look through the pages and let your imagination wander. In collage, there are no rules!

An old jewelry box can hold wonderful treasures for creating cards. This old cameo was the perfect centerpiece for this "antiquey" card. I added bits of lace, ribbon roses. and segments from an old costume pearl necklace, purchased at a flea market.

Stickers and Decals

Stickers and decals are available in most any type of art, craft, variety or card shop. They come in a multitude of sizes and shapes, and they're not just for kids. You can find, for example, beautiful Victorian florals that make very sophisticated gifts.

Using stickers or decals is, by far, the fastest, easiest way to trim napkins and table place cards for parties, create simple cards, or add festivity to just about anything you use in everyday living. For the holiday card below, I used a simple rub-on decal and dressed it up with a few droplets of dimensional paint.

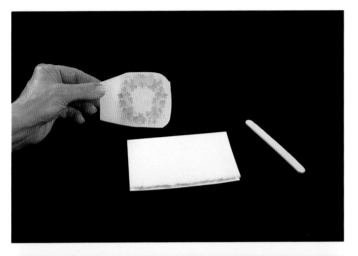

1 Choose the rub-on transfer you wish to use. Carefully peel off the backing and place the transfer face down on your card surface.

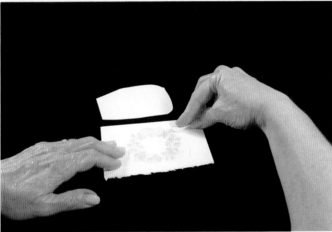

2 Using a craft stick, tongue depressor or coin, rub firmly. Be sure to rub down all areas of the image. Carefully peel off the paper.

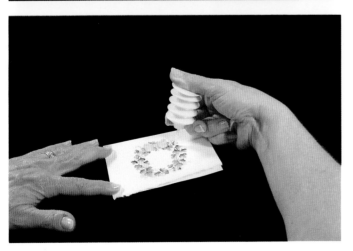

3 Embellish with droplets of paint from a squeeze bottle. You can also apply paint dots with a toothpick, stylus, or the end of a brush handle. Here I added little light green berries and a few beads of metallic gold glitter paint.

These adorable snowmen were simply "recycled" from a scrap of used gift wrap. After gluing them to a fresh piece of construction paper, I embellished the image with artificial snow and a touch of acrylic paint.

Scraps of fabric and a bit of dimensional outlining paint can result in an amazing collection of cards. Having trouble drawing your own patterns? Try tracing shapes from cookie cutters.

This variation of the window card employs an elaborate (yet easy to use) Victorian sticker. I played up the theme by trimming the window with a bit of old lace.

Check your sewing kit for recyclable scraps of fabric, or purchase a couple of remnants from a fabric store. To avoid glue seepage on this card, I applied white glue to cardboard, then squeegeed off the excess with a scrap of cardboard before applying the cloth.

Taking the time to create a soft cloth keepsake can be very rewarding. This matching fabric gift ensemble was perfect for a new baby gift. For more on fabric collage, turn to the next page.

Fabric

When I was privileged to visit Russia, I bought many items made of cloth, including greeting and note cards. The Russians are extremely frugal people. Many materials are not yet available, so fabrics from old clothes are saved and used in marvelous ways.

You can purchase remnant scraps of cloth at any quilt, fabric or hobby shop. The array of textures, colors and patterns in old fabric swatches is endless, and beautiful cards can be created with a little glue and some imagination. The clever 3-D stocking below and the sumptuous velvet card on the following pages are just two examples of the endless effects you can achieve with fabric.

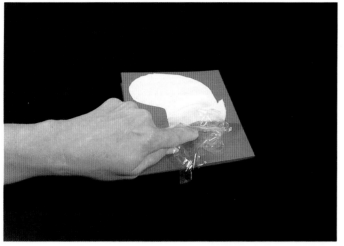

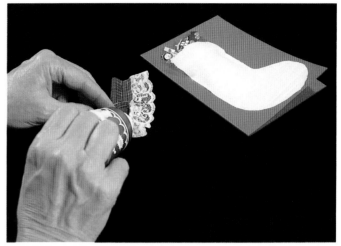

1 Cut a stocking shape from muslin or any other fabric. Apply white glue to the edges of the stocking shape and press it onto your card. Leave the top open. Stuff the top with a piece of crumpled plastic wrap to give it dimension. Then glue a few toys in place in the top of the stocking to create an "overflowing" effect.

2 To make the trim, fold a piece of fabric in half over the edge of a scrap of lace and glue it in place. Once dry, cut the trim so that it is the same width as the top of the stocking. Glue it in place at the mouth of the stocking. Add more baubles and trinkets as you wish.

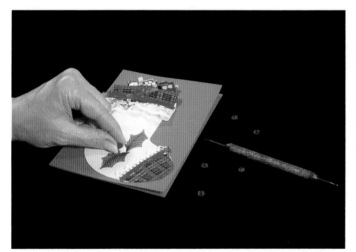

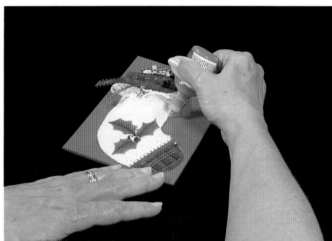

3 Trim the toe of the stocking with the same fabric used for the top. Then, add finishing touches. Here, I cut some holly leaves out of a scrap of holly-printed cotton and glued them down. Red rhinestone jewels made perfect holly berries. I dropped white glue beads onto the leaves and pressed the berries gently into place with a stylus.

4 Jazz up the card and hide any frayed edges by outlining the entire stocking with dimensional writing paint. Be sure to shake out all the bubbles in the squeeze bottle before applying the paint directly to your card.

This wonderful nostalgic card was created out of old jewelry, fabric and lace to make a frameable keepsake. This type of card never turns out the same. The surprise element can be lots of fun.

1 Cut a heavy piece of cardboard to the desired card size. Next, cut a piece of velvet approximately 1 inch larger than the cardboard on all sides. Miter the corners and clip away the excess fabric from the corners.

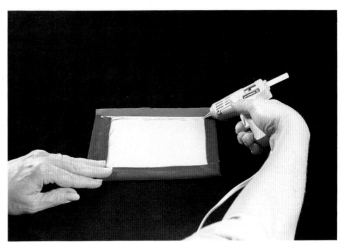

2 Fold the edges of the fabric over the card and glue in place on the back of the card using a low-temp glue gun or household glue. Allow the edges to dry completely.

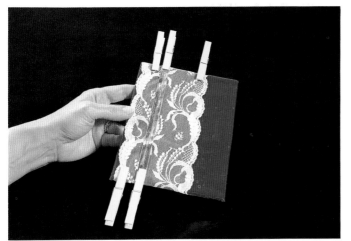

3 Dress up the front of the card with more layers of fabric, lace or ribbon. I used a wide scrap of lace and gold ribbon, simply folding the edges over and gluing them onto the back. Clothespins are perfect for holding trim in place while drying.

4 To hide the glued ribbon ends on the back of the card, cut a piece of velvet the exact size of the card. Glue it in place over top of the stray ends. If you wish to write a message on the back of the card, simply cover the back with paper or cardboard instead of fabric.

5 Returning to the front, cut a new shape from cardboard (I chose a heart). Cover it with fabric (see Step 1), mitering the corners and folding them over and gluing in place on the back of the shape. Here, I covered my heart shape with red velvet for contrast.

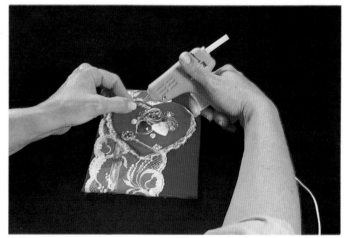

6 Trim the heart by gluing lace to the back. Allow the lace to extend over the edges of the heart. Use a pencil or stylus to hold the lace in place as you are gluing.

7 Once the lace is dry, flip the heart over. (It's not necessary to cover the back with cloth. It won't be seen.) Embellish the heart surface, adding charms or old jewelry with a low-temp glue gun. To finish, glue the heart to the front of the card.

Lace and Ribbon

As the whimsical card below shows, ribbon can be used in fanciful ways. This summery treat was created simply by looping ribbon repeatedly and gluing in place with a low-temp glue gun. The cone pattern was traced from a store-bought stencil and outlined with dimensional glitter paint.

Additionally, some of the most elegant and feminine cards can be created with just a touch of lace, ribbon and some silk flowers. When I was married,

my mother gave me a beautiful wedding card made from a piece of lace from my grandmother's wedding dress. The card is framed and hangs in our bedroom—a "forever" keepsake.

The following projects will enable you to create perfect cards for weddings, bridal showers, anniversaries, sweet sixteens, Mother's Day and a variety of other occasions.

Dimensional cards are fun to design and can become lasting keepsakes. They are lovely framed and placed on a table or desk for all to view and enjoy. I chose an antique white stock as the base for this feminine wedding gift.

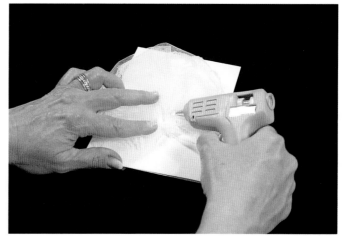

1 Create or purchase a card 5″×7″ in dimension. Next, cut a piece of tulle 6″×18″ and a piece of lace 3″×12″. Fold the tulle in half. With a needle and thread, weave the needle in and out through the tulle approximately ¼ inch from the raw edge. Gather the tulle tightly on the thread and make a couple of stitches to hold it in place. Repeat the process with the lace, only don't fold the lace in half.

2 Using a low-temp glue gun and generous amounts of glue, attach the lace to the center of the card; then glue the tulle over top of it.

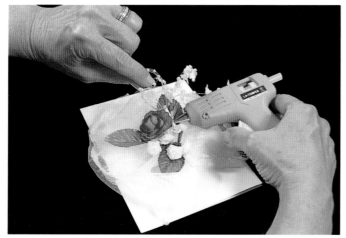

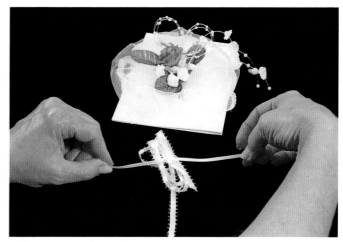

3 Embellish with silk flowers, leaves and pearls on monofilament line. (These items can be purchased at your local craft or fabric store.)

4 Create a bow by wrapping silk ribbon around your fingers several times (use two fingers for a small bow, three for a larger bow). Remove the loops from your fingers and tie the loops in the middle. Ruffle the loops into bloom and glue the bow onto the card. To finish the card, adhere pearls at random to hide any raw edges.

Fabric stiffener is an extremely heavy starch that can be
used to mold fabric and lace into different shapes. It dries
clear. The molded fan shape on this card was a perfect base
for a feminine Mother's Day sentiment.

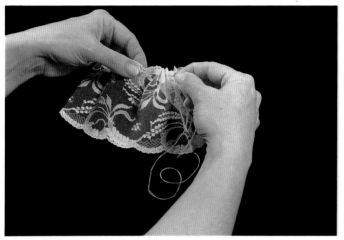

1 With a needle and thread, gather a piece of lace in the same way as shown on page 23.

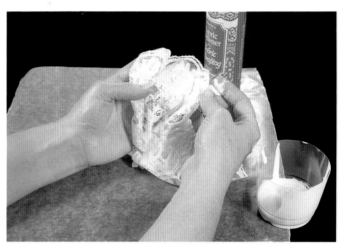

2 Generously coat the lace with fabric stiffener, working the stiffener through with your fingers. Blot any excess stiffening agent from the lace.

3 On wax paper, form the lace into the shape of a fan, turning the raw edges under. The stiffening agent will turn clear when dry.

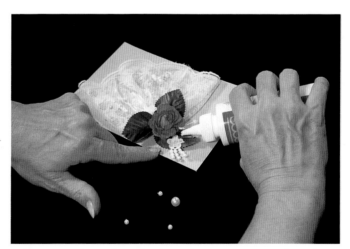

4 Once dry, glue the lace fan to your card and accent with silk flowers, leaves and pearl trinkets. Use a low-temp glue gun or white glue to attach your accessories.

Pressed Flowers

Pick fresh flowers in the spring and summer, press them and save them for a rainy day. Keep a cache of pressed flowers and you can make beautiful, natural looking cards all year round. A beautiful, preserved flower can bring a burst of cheer to any gloomy, winter day.

Dried blossoms and buds are also ideal for keepsakes. I saved flowers from our daughter's wedding, pressed them, and used them to make a card for her first anniversary. She loved the card so much that she framed it.

Remember also that you can use different flowers to send a wide variety of messages. Pansies symbolize "thinking of you." Violets represent "longing for friends." Columbine signifies "lion-like courage." Consult your local florist for more information on the symbolic meaning of different types of flowers.

To accompany the card below, I made a see-through envelope. What better way to showcase beautiful flowers?

To press flowers:

1 Select flowers and leaves in different stages of bloom. Carefully arrange them on blotter paper or paper towels and press between heavy books for two to three weeks (phone books or dictionaries work well). Be sure the flowers and leaves are completely dry before removing them. If they are damp they may mildew or fall apart.

To create a card:

2 Neatly arrange the flowers and foliage on your card to create a pleasing design. Once your arrangement is set, anchor it in place with a thick, clear-drying glue.

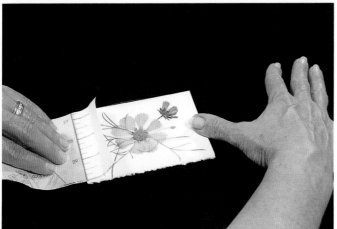

3 To preserve and protect the arrangement, you may wish to cover it with contact paper, as we've done here. For a more open, natural look, spray the arrangement with a few coats of clear acrylic sealer. Tip: Hair spray works as an effective sealant too!

To make the clear envelope:

4 Photocopy the envelope pattern on the adjacent page and enlarge it to the desired size. Or, for quicker results, simply unseam a store-bought envelope and use it as a pattern. Trace the pattern onto a piece of clear acetate with a grease pencil. (I used an acetate report cover, but you can buy whole sheets of acetate if you wish.) Cut out the pattern with scissors or a utility knife. Then, fold the envelope at the dotted fold lines, scoring the edges with a stylus. Remove any grease pencil lines with glass cleaner.

5 Fold the envelope up with the card inside. (Here, we've shown the envelope without the card for easier viewing.) Next, simply seal the envelope with a sticker or some sealing wax. I melted several drops of sealing wax onto the envelope flap and made a unique imprint with the face of an old button.

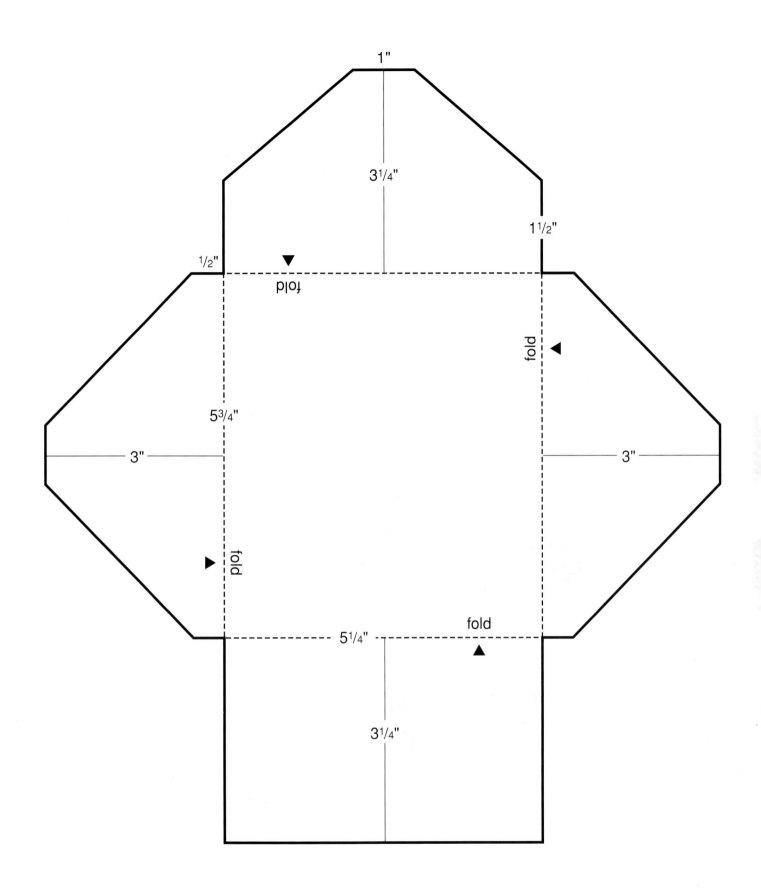

1"

3¹/₄"

1¹/₂"

¹/₂"

▼

fold

fold

◄

5³/₄"

3"

3"

► fold

fold

▲

5¹/₄"

3¹/₄"

A deckled-edge card creates the background for a wildflower wreath glued together with little pieces of lacy fern.

This thank-you note with matching envelope was made with pressed flowers from the bouquets of the bride and bridesmaids. The flowers were enjoyed long after the wedding was over.

Don't ever throw away scraps of paper. You can use them to make gift enclosure cards. This scrap of handmade paper, adorned with cosmos and larkspur, made a perfect tie-on. Punch a hole in the corner, add a little ribbon, and it's just beautiful.

Blank window cards can be found in art, craft, needlework and stationery stores. The basket for this charming wildflower arrangement is cut from a flat piece of cork.

Mixed Media "Junk" Cards

"Junk cards," as we called them when I was growing up, can be made from just about anything around the house: scraps of paper, leftover gift wrappings, beads, trinkets, and other "found" objects that might otherwise be discarded.

The cards showcased on the following pages prove that with a little creativity, frugality and resourcefulness, you can make a charming gift for any occasion with almost anything.

That's right! The pocket of old blue jeans trimmed with a little lace, buttons, bangles and beads creates a memory of days gone by. Try to get your hands on a few personal items from the past belonging to a family member or special friend. You'll thrill the person receiving the card.

Behind the oval of this window card, I glued a sheet of copper to enhance the clear angel charm hanging in front. Silk roses, pearls and lace were added for antique effect.

A nice way to use beautiful old crocheted doilies is to transform them into greeting cards. Embellish the card with ribbons, charms and beads.

Lace paper doilies, floral gift wrapping paper and ribbon were used to make this wonderful card with matching envelope. The envelope used as a base is simply a business-sized variety, purchased from the grocery store.

A straw hat trimmed with ribbons and artificial flowers is a splendid party invitation. Don't worry about the depth of the hat — we tried it and it came through the mail beautifully.

An invitation to a concert, perhaps? How about a musical recital? Personalizing a card for a special event or party adds a touch that cannot be bought in a store.

Scraps from a paper doily, spray painted gold, created a whole new look for this cherub, recycled from a used Christmas card.

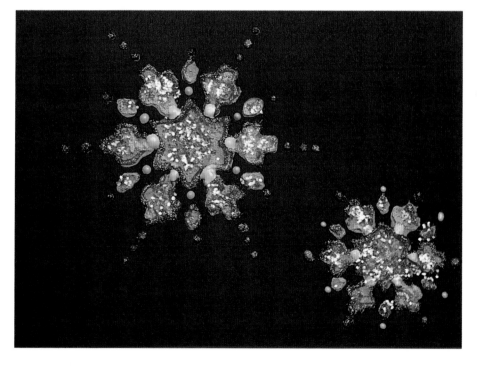

Dark paper stock gives a very dramatic look to a card. These snowflakes were traced from a stencil and embellished with glitter paint. The card is perfect as an invitation to a winter ball.

Chapter Three

PRINTMAKING

I f you wish to produce a large number of cards in a short period of time, consider printing. With one print block or stamp, you can produce a whole stack of attractive cards or a matching gift ensemble in no time. This method is perfect for Christmas cards, graduation announcements, invitations and place cards.

Almost everyone makes a potato print at some point in their childhood, but the truth is, printmaking isn't just for kids. You'll find in this chapter that many different effects can be achieved with prints, as there are a multitude of objects and materials that can be used. By expanding your horizons to other types of vegetables, household items, store-bought stamps and craft supplies, you can arrive at some highly sophisticated designs.

Print blocks are most often made either by carving a found object such as a potato or bar of soap, or by using an object directly as is, such as the tip of a celery stalk. You can also use a wide variety of manufactured stamps and ink pads.

The projects in this chapter can be categorized into two types of prints: positive prints and negative, or reverse prints. A positive print is made by applying paint to the surface of an object and pressing the object onto paper or some other surface. Conversely, a negative print is made by laying the object on the paper and painting around the outside of the object.

Flat, dehydrated sponges can be cut in a variety of shapes. Once hydrated, the shapes make perfect printing tools. All of the elements for this Southwestern gift wrap were cut and printed from sponges.

Rubber Stamps and Rollers

Rubber stamps present one of the easiest routes to making multiple, printed cards. These clever, quick, inexpensive items can be found in your local art, craft and stationery stores, and sometimes even in grocery stores. They come in endless varieties too: stars, suns, moons, flowers, animals, cartoon characters, trees, mountains, hearts, dinosaurs, quilt designs, border designs—you name it.

To create the adorable teddy bear card below, I added accents to an ordinary ink stamp with a little watercolor and some ribbon. The result was a one-of-a-kind creation.

Rolling stamps with interchangeable rubber cartridges can be purchased at most major craft stores. With a stamp roller, you can make stationery, gift enclosures and note cards quickly and easily with little or no mess.

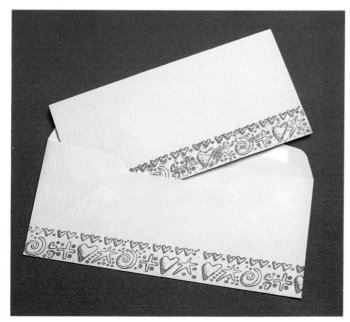

With a stamp roller, you can trim the edges of plain paper and envelopes to create matching stationery.

The "bubble" cartridge for the stamp roller is one of my favorites. Here, I used two different ink pads, in pink and purple, to transform an ordinary sack into a charming gift bag.

Reverse or Negative Prints

To print in reverse, simply place an object on your paper and paint around it. When the object is lifted, a reverse image, or negative space, will be left on the paper.

Flyspecking creates a soft, pebbly effect and will allow you to create beautiful reverse prints without smearing or smudging. All you need is a toothbrush, some heavy card stock, any kind of paint and a steady hand. For this card, I used a combination of acrylics in dioxazine purple, phthalo green and cerulean blue, but of course you can be creative and come up with your own color harmonies. Be sure to water down your paints before you begin. For more on flyspecking, turn to page 7.

1 Choose an object (I used a silk leaf) and lightly trace around it onto heavy paper or card stock to create your design. For this card, I used a piece of 140-lb. watercolor paper. Once your design is set, put the leaf down on the paper.

2 Load your toothbrush with a thin wash of acrylic. Pull your thumb over the bristles to speckle the paint onto the paper (you might want to practice first on a separate piece of paper). Carefully move the leaf to another area on the card and repeat the process with a different paint color.

3 Once your flyspecks are dry, thin out your paint washes a little more. Using a flat brush, float some color around the outside edges of the leaves to make the negative shapes pop out. Allow the color washes to overlap and blend.

4 Once the washes have dried, use a liner brush with more wash to paint in the veins on the leaves. Add finishing touches by lining the edge of the card with a felt-tip marker.

Positive Prints

Positive prints can be made with almost any found object. Simply paint directly on the object and press the object face down on paper. I like to use fresh leaves whenever possible for printing. They are flexible and come in all shapes and sizes. For this project, I used warm acrylic cadmiums in red, orange and yellow, plus burnt sienna to create an earthy, autumn design. I also added copper highlights for seasonal flair. Brown paper raffia and silk leaves were perfect accessories for the finished, wrapped box.

1 First, choose the leaves you will print with. Make sure they aren't too dry, or they may crumble. With a flat brush, apply generous amounts of paint to one leaf in patches, overlapping colors haphazardly. Turn the leaf over and place in the desired location on the paper.

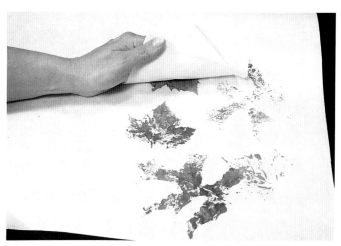

2 Cover the leaf with an absorbent tissue or paper towel and press firmly on all edges to ensure that the paint is transferred to the paper.

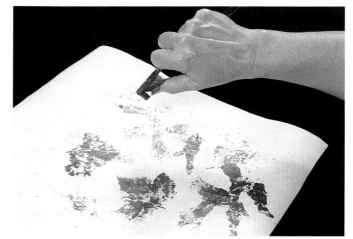

3 Once you've printed all your large leaf shapes, thin out your paint colors with water and flyspeck around the leaves with a toothbrush for added sparkle. (For more on flyspecking, turn to pages 7 and 41.)

Vegetable Prints

With a little imagination, the most ordinary household items can be used to create beautiful designs. Half the fun of the gift set below is telling people that I used celery to make it. They are always surprised. Who would have guessed that the end of a celery stalk is the perfect shape for a rose petal?

For this project, I used acrylic paints directly out of the tube, creating a mixture of porcelain pink, magenta and raspberry. The thick paint adhered well to the celery stalks and maintained a rich color. Instead of using only one piece of celery, I chose several stalks and cut them at different points. Each end created a different size petal.

1 Dip the end of your celery stalk in the paint and blot it on a rag. Then, press it firmly onto your paper. It helps to begin with the smallest pieces, building the center of the rose first. Increase the size of your petals as you work toward the outside of the rose.

2 To render the leaves, paint the surface of an actual celery leaf. I used Hooker's green.

3 Place the leaf face down onto the paper surface. Cover it with a paper towel and press firmly. Carefully lift away the towel, then the leaf.

4 To add a touch of charm, thin out your paint and add curlicues or squiggles with a liner brush. Then, using the same paint washes, flyspeck around the rose for a shimmering effect. Once the card is dry, brush on a coat of gold glitter paint. The paint will dry clear, leaving a glittery sparkle to your finished piece.

Sponge Prints

One of the most versatile printing tools is the sponge. Flat, dehydrated sponges (often called magic sponges) can be bought in craft stores and cut into a variety of shapes and sizes. To create this bright, cheery gift wrap, I cut several watermelon shapes from a flat sponge and knocked out a whole roll of summery paper in less than an hour.

To capture the brightness of a juicy melon, I used acrylic colors in permanent green light, cadmium red light and white. For contrast in the seeds, I used shiny black dimensional paint.

1 Cut pieces of flat sponge to resemble watermelon slices. Be sure to leave a "bite" out of one or two of the slices for fun. Wet the sponge pieces and squeeze out the excess water. Next, using a large, flat brush, paint the rind and melon directly on the sponge with acrylics. Don't paint the seeds onto the sponge. Save those for later.

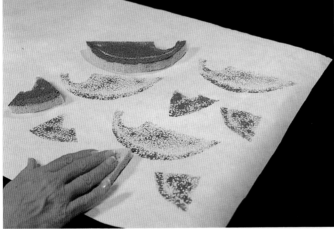

2 After a few practice runs on scrap paper, begin printing your gift wrap by painting the sponge pieces, then pressing them face down on the paper. I used butcher paper for this project, but have used brown paper and even newspaper in the past.

3 Once the printed melon slices are dry, paint on the seeds with a no. 1 watercolor brush and generous strokes of shiny black acrylic paint. Stagger the placement of the seeds. If you wish, create a gift set by printing a matching card.

Many variations of sponge painting can be used in creating wrapping papers. For this holiday wrap, I simply traced a Christmas tree shape from a cookie cutter onto a flat sponge, cut out the shape, and printed with it. I then ornamented the trees with red pompoms. Cinnamon candies or red jewels could also be glued in place for a similar effect.

To create this festive Christmas gift wrap, I traced around a cookie cutter on brown butcher paper, then outlined the shapes with shiny brown dimensional paint and added glitter. A matching card—cut from the same cookie cutter pattern—added just the right touch.

Eraser Prints

Yet another object that lends itself well to printing is an eraser. Erasers can be carved easily and are extremely durable. Plus, they are advantageous in that they are nonperishable. You can easily leave this project and pick it up later. With vegetable and leaf prints, you have to work quickly before your printing materials wilt!

It's best to use a soft Artgum eraser that won't crumble when carved. Because the eraser surface will be small, choose a design that is fairly simple—preferably a single shape. You can always carve several erasers in different shapes and use them all on one card if you wish. For this refreshingly simple Valentine's card and matching envelope, one shape was adequate.

To make the card:

1 First, draw your design on the surface of the eraser or transfer a found design onto the eraser with carbon paper. Using a sharp utility knife, make an incision around the design about ¼-inch deep.

2 Cut in from the sides of the eraser toward the design, carefully removing small pieces of the eraser until the design pops up from the surface.

3 With a flat brush, paint the design surface with an acrylic color straight from the tube. I used a rich cadmium red medium. Turn the eraser over and firmly press the design surface onto paper. Repaint the design surface after each application, if needed.

4 I created a bouquet of heart shapes, then added stems and leaves with a green felt-tip marking pen.

To make the heart envelope:

5 Photocopy the envelope pattern at right and enlarge to your desired size. Transfer the pattern onto a stiff, durable paper such as watercolor paper; then cut it out using scissors or a utility knife. Using a ruler as a guide, score the fold lines with a stylus or some other object (such as a pen cap or the blunt end of a crochet needle).

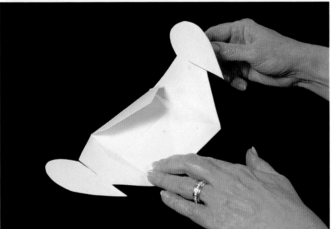

6 Fold the envelope flaps inward on all four sides, beginning with the bottom flap, then the top, then the sides.

7 Latch the two heart halves together on the side flaps. Decorate by printing a heart bouquet on the outside of the envelope.

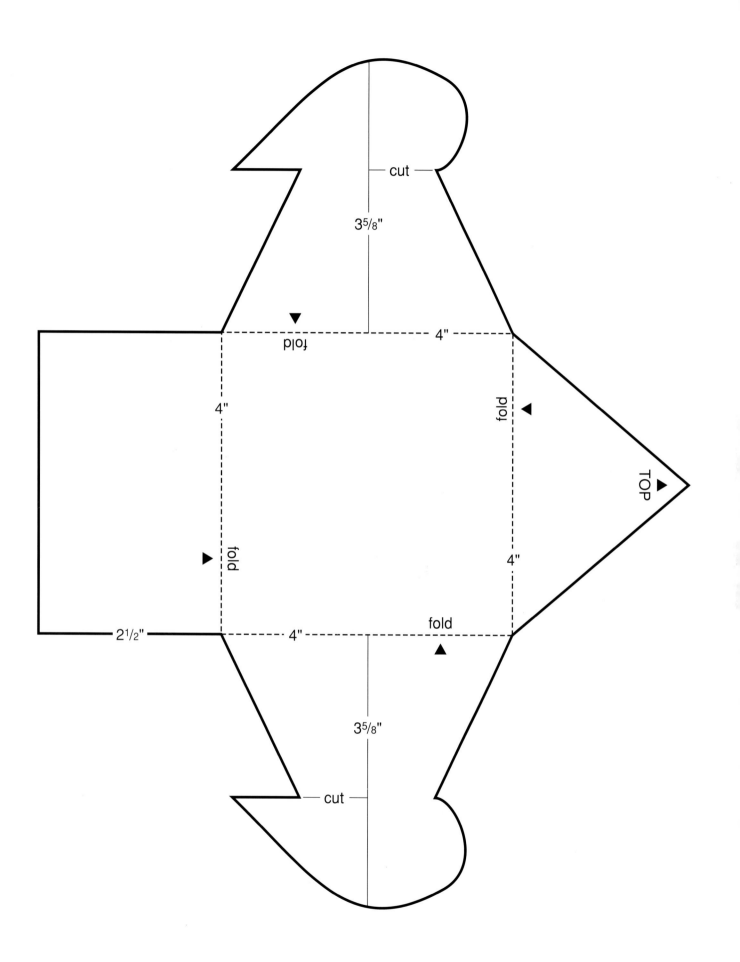

cut

$3^{5}/_{8}$"

fold

4"

4"

fold

fold

TOP

4"

fold

2$^{1}/_{2}$"

4"

$3^{5}/_{8}$"

cut

Styrofoam Prints

Styrofoam is another household item that can be carved easily into adorable shapes for printing. This clever, easy-to-assemble party invitation was a big hit! Using metallic acrylics for extra flair and pizzazz, I transformed plain black construction paper into a jazzy invitation. The finishing touch was the packaging: Instead of sending the usual envelope, I dressed up some simple mailing tubes, rolled the invitations inside and added party favors and glittery confetti.

To create the Styrofoam letter blocks, you can either draw the letters directly on the Styrofoam or make them first on paper. The easiest, mistake-free method is to draw a letter first on paper, cut it out, flip it so it is reversed, and trace it onto the Styrofoam block. If you choose to draw directly on the block, be sure to draw in reverse (mirror) so that the letter will face the proper direction when printed.

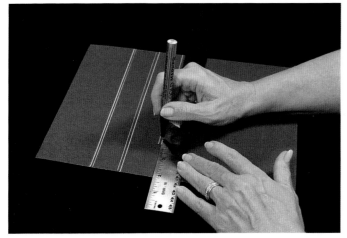

1 With a pencil, draw spacing lines for your lettering on black construction paper. Using a cork-backed ruler as a guide, retrace the lines with gold and silver metallic markers. These lines will serve as guides when you print your letters.

2 Draw or trace your letters onto Styrofoam cubes (one letter per cube). With a sharp utility knife, cut into each cube at least ¼-inch down. Then cut from the side inward, chipping out small pieces of Styrofoam until the letter surface pops out.

3 Using a flat brush, apply a generous amount of paint to the raised surface of the letter. Flip the printing block over and press firmly onto your paper. *Be sure your letters are facing the right direction before you print!* Rock the Styrofoam back and forth gently to make certain the entire letter is printing. Once all the letters have been printed, dress up the image with triangles, squares and other shapes (also cut from Styrofoam). Then outline the letters and shapes with metallic marking pens. Finish the invitation by hand, writing the party details in metallic pen.

Soap Prints

Soap is yet another household item which, when carved creatively, becomes a perfect print block. Choose a soap or beauty bar that is relatively soft and easy to work with. A hard lye soap may crumble and break easily.

Kokopeli, a symbol of mischief and abundance in Southwest mythology, was the perfect subject for this whimsical, all-occasion set of note cards. The character is very popular and can be found in many design books. I cut the silhouette for this design from a magazine.

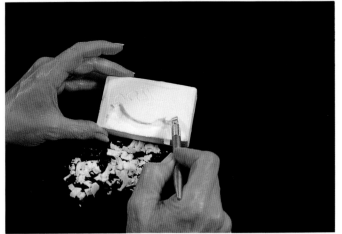

1 Plane off any indentations in the soap (such as the brand name) leaving a smooth surface. Place your design face down on the soap and trace around it with a stylus or some other pointed object. Your tracing marks should leave an indentation in the soap.

2 Remove the tracing paper and carefully cut away the soap surrounding the design. Be sure to carve away the soap in small chunks. You don't want to accidentally remove part of your design. When you finish carving, your design should pop up approximately ¼-inch higher than the rest of the soap bar.

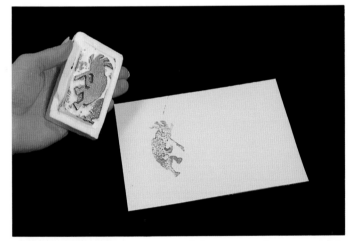

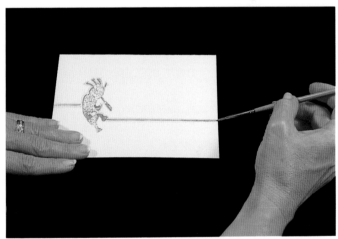

3 Apply paint to the raised design on the soap with a flat brush. Flip the soap block and press it onto your card. Don't press too hard; soap is fragile and may break.

4 Accent the design with silver metallic pen. First measure off your lines in pencil, then ink the lines using a ruler as a guide. To finish, I added a stripe of copper paint down the center of two silver lines using a liner brush. Then, I repeated the whole process to create a matching envelope.

Chapter Four

INKING AND PAINTING

Compared to some of the other projects in this book, painting may be a little messier and a little more time-consuming. But one thing it is *not* is more difficult. Each time I teach a workshop, my beginning students fear the idea of even picking up a paintbrush. The truth is, you don't have to be Michelangelo to paint.

The world is full of designs waiting to be traced and painted in new, exciting ways. Try looking through clip art books, magazines and other printed materials for traceable designs. Also, don't forget that cookie cutters and store-bought stencils are perfect for copying simple, bold shapes. Traced designs can be as easy to paint as coloring book images.

You may notice that many of the projects in other chapters of this book involve paint in some form or another. This chapter will explore even more options for what you can do with paint. Some projects in this chapter don't even involve brushwork. Sponges and other household objects can be substituted for paintbrushes quite easily.

Explore the different effects you can achieve with different types of paints, papers, tools and techniques. For most of the projects in this chapter, you'll need a fair amount of space in a well-ventilated area, especially if you're working with oils. Be sure to wear old clothes. Some of the projects can be messy.

Marbleizing is an elegant technique that can be used to create an assortment of gifts, from note cards, to bookmarks, to package tie-ons. To see how it's done, turn to pages 72-75.

Eraser Painting

One of the easiest ways to alleviate "fear of painting" is to get away from the brush altogether. Experiment with different household items and paint applicators. For example, a pencil eraser produces an interesting effect in acrylics.

This delicate and romantic card is one of my favorites. After twisting on the roses with a pencil eraser, I sponged on some green leaves. Stems were later applied using a thin liner brush.

Sponge Brushes

Sponges come in brush form and can also be used to create interesting effects in acrylic. Here, the sponge brush was a perfect shape for dainty flower petals.

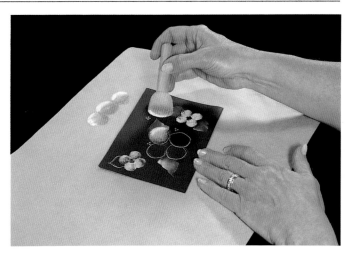

Round sponge brushes in different sizes were also used to create flowers, berries and grapes. I later glued on plastic jewels and embellished this card with dimensional paint.

Cellophane Scrunching

This texturing technique can be applied to any well-sealed surface and creates an interesting effect. It works particularly well when combined with a surface coated in gold or silver leaf (as was the case with the box below). To learn more about metallic leafing, turn to pages 98-103.

1 Apply metallic leaf to the paper or cardboard surface as described on pages 101-102. Burnish the leaf. Then seal the surface with a few thin coats of acrylic spray. Note: You don't have to work with metallic leaf. A glossy, coated paper stock will work equally well for this technique.

2 Using a sponge, apply oil color (mixed with a little turpentine) over top of the leaf.

3 Press a crumpled piece of plastic wrap into the wet oil color and lift. The result will be a crackled, crystallized surface.

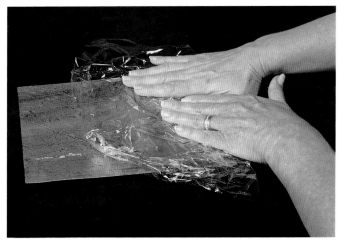

Inking

Inking is easier than it sounds. Simply trace a pattern onto your card stock in pencil, then retrace the lines with an ink pen.

A touch of oil wash on inked vellum creates a gentle, transparent effect—almost like a stained glass window. The technique was perfect for these pre-cious holiday cards. Rather than drawing from scratch, I traced the line drawings for these two cards from a clip art book. After inking the designs, I added transparent oil washes of alizarin crimson, Prussian blue and cadmium yellow light.

1 Cut a piece of vellum to the desired size and fold in half to create a card. Place your design inside the card and close the card. The design will show through the vellum.

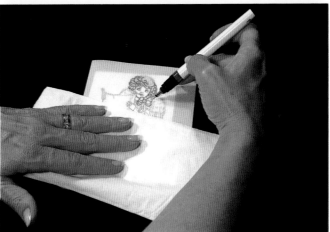

2 Using a black ink technical pen (I used a size 0), trace the design onto the front of the vellum card. Place a tissue under your hand to avoid smearing the ink while you work.

3 Squeeze the oil colors of your choice onto a palette and thin them with turpentine. I like to use transparent colors to push the glass effect. Next, simply paint within your ink lines—like filling in a coloring book. Deepen some of the shadowed areas with thicker washes of paint. Once the initial paint layer is dry, accent the image by applying white dots of paint (straight from the tube) with a toothpick.

Combining Techniques

To dress up this zany, extra-large shopping bag, I combined straight brushwork in acrylics with sponge painting and a few other craft techniques. For this project, do not thin your paint colors. Use them straight from the tube for maximum punch.

Vegetables can be a lot of fun as subjects and are easy to render with brushes and sponges. I chose carrots as a theme because they're simple to render. The heavy brown bag combined with cadmium orange paint resulted in a smart autumn ensemble. The project was a lot of fun and was a big hit as a gift bag.

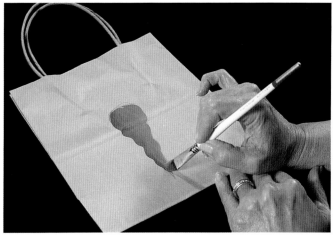

1 Draw a carrot (an elongated teardrop shape) on your paper bag. Using a large, synthetic brush, fill in the shape with cadmium orange paint. To add dimension, shade one side of the carrot with burnt sienna. Highlight the opposite side with a touch of cadmium yellow light.

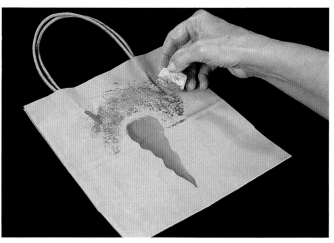

2 Dip a small scrap of sponge in leaf green paint and dab above the carrot to create foliage. Pick up a little yellow with the sponge and add highlights to the leaves.

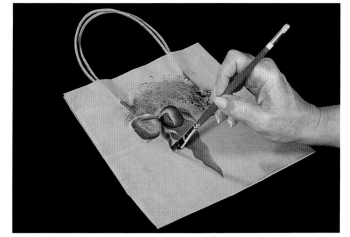

3 Once the carrot is dry, paint a bow and streamers over top of it. Load a flat brush on one side with dioxazine purple, on the other side with titanium white. Twist the brush as you paint the bow to blend the colors.

Masking

Masking makes it easy to paint sloppily without ruining any white space on the card. For this charming window card, I created a checkerboard pattern simply by taping wherever I didn't want the paint to go. This card is perfect for Valentine's Day, baby showers, or as an all-occasion card.

When using tape for masking purposes, be sure to use quilting tape, drafting tape or nonstick painter's tape. Regular masking tape may adhere too strongly and rip the card when removed.

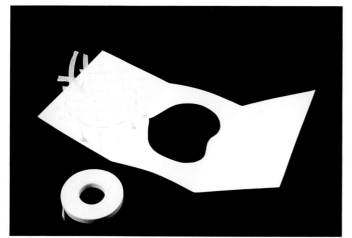

1 Make a trifold card and cut a heart-shaped window in the center section. Fold the card and trace the heart shape through the window. Then unfold the card so that the traced outline is facing up. Mask out a diagonal grid pattern across the heart with tape. (You may want to draw in guidelines with a ruler and pencil before applying the tape.)

2 Using acrylic paints straight from the tube and a synthetic brush, paint the squares on the heart shape diagonally in rows. I used soft pastels in permanent blue light, porcelain pink and light violet. Allow the paint to dry completely. Then, gently remove the tape.

3 Using blue dimensional paint with a fine-line applicator, outline each paint square on the heart. Be sure to shake the dimensional paint down into the nozzle to get rid of air bubbles before you begin outlining.

4 Accent by gluing a piece of lace ribbon to the inside of the heart window. Use a stylus to hold the lace in place as you are gluing.

Marbleizing

Marbleizing is extremely elegant and impressive, yet is amazingly fast and simple. In one session, you can easily produce a whole set of note cards, invitations, bookmarks or stationery. It's impossible to predict how the colorful swirls will turn out ahead of time, but it's always exciting to see the endless color combinations and shapes that arise by chance.

Marbleizing is done with oil paints and turpentine, and consequently can be messy. You'll need a fair amount of space in a well-ventilated area. Try to avoid working in the kitchen if possible. It's best to keep craft materials—especially toxic ones—separate from cooking utensils and food. Use plastic dispos-

able containers for your paints. Avoid using Styrofoam; the turpentine will eat right through it.

You can use any kind of paper to marbleize and can create a multitude of color combinations. For this project, I used oil colors in phthalo green and Prussian blue. It usually works best to mix colors that are close to each other in the spectrum. Other pleasant combinations are Indian yellow/phthalo green and alizarin crimson/Prussian blue. Have fun creating your own combinations. Just be aware that mixing complementary colors (such as red/green or blue/orange) may produce a muddy brown.

1 In small, plastic disposable containers, thin your oil colors with odorless turpentine. A drop of paint the size of a pea should be mixed with approximately 3 tablespoons of turpentine.

2 Mix your colors with a wooden craft stick or other disposable tool. Your mix should have the consistency of a thin wash, yet should appear opaque. Adjust the paint/turp ratio until you've achieved this effect.

3 Pour a few drops of each color into a large aluminum baking pan of water. The paint should coagulate into droplets on the surface of the water. Be careful not to add too much paint, or you'll have to start over. The water surface should not be completely filmed over with paint.

4 Using a palette knife or craft stick, swirl the oil colors together on the water surface.

5 Make handles out of masking tape and attach the tape to the back of the paper you wish to marbleize. Be sure the tape is firmly secured. Then, grasping the tape handles, gently float the front of the paper on the water surface. (If you wish to marbleize the edge of a card on both sides, simply dip the edge straight down into the water.)

6 Lift straight up and you will find a beautiful, different design on your paper each time. Let the paper dry for several days.

NOTE: *Marbleizing can be tricky the first time you try it. You may have to play with the paint consistency a bit to get the desired effect. Too much turpentine in the mix will result in thin, dull, washed-out color. On the other hand, if you have too much paint and not enough turp, the paint won't spread on the water and will produce large, flat globs of color on the paper. Be patient and experiment. The end result will be well worth it!*

Beautiful gift sets and stationery can be created using the marbleizing technique. These items were created using a combination of phthalo green and Prussian blue oil color.

Stenciling

Stencils provide a quick and easy alternative for decorating cards, and the results are clean and professional looking. Fabulous stencils are available in craft stores, or you can design and cut your own. Special brushes are manufactured for stenciling purposes. The bristles are stiff and work well for scrubbing.

To create this exotic card, I used a simple fan stencil with metallic paint and added flair with a metallic tassel.

To make the card:

1 Cut a piece of rice paper and a sheet of gold tissue paper the same size. Fold both in half. Deckle one edge of the rice paper (for deckled edge demonstration, turn to page 8). Spray the inside of the rice paper with a thin coat of clear acrylic and adhere the tissue paper to the inside.

2 Position the stencil on the outside of the card and secure in place with a piece of quilting, drafting, or other nonstick tape.

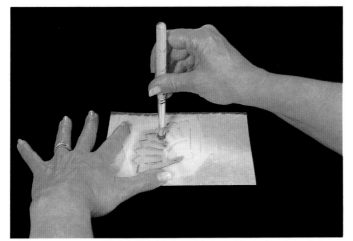

3 Using a stiff, round stencil brush, pick up some paint and gently scrub the paint into the holes in the stencil using a circular motion. To match the gold tissue paper, I used gold metallic acrylic paint.

4 After you've removed the stencil and the paint is dry, outline the shape left by the stencil with a silver metallic liner pen.

To make the tassel:

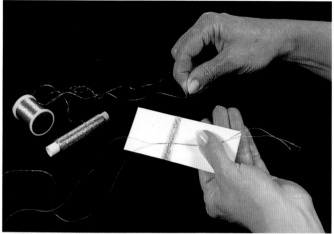

5 Cut a small piece of cardboard (roughly 2 inches wide) and wrap gold and silver twine around it multiple times.

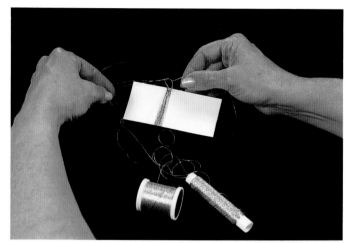

6 Tie the loose ends of the twine in several knots, then cut the loose ends about 3 inches above the knots, leaving long strands.

7 Pull the loops off the cardboard and wrap the long strands around one end of the loops. Knot securely.

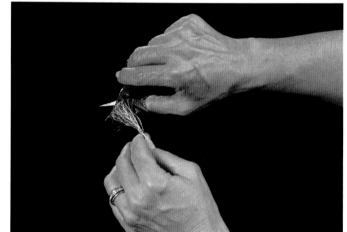

8 Slip scissors through the loops on the opposite end and cut the loops apart. Glue the tassel to the front of the card.

To make a matching envelope:

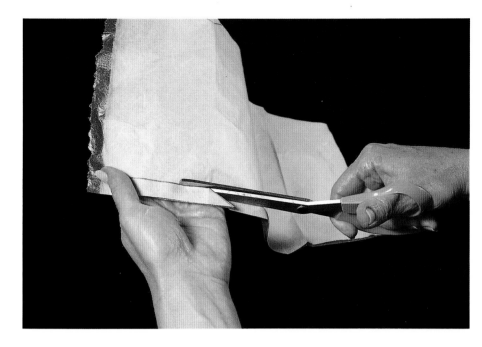

9 Using spray mount adhesive, glue together a sheet of rice paper and a sheet of gold tissue paper. Choose a store-bought envelope in the size you want and carefully take it apart at the seams. Trace the opened envelope onto the rice paper side. Cut out the envelope shape from the rice/tissue paper.

10 Fold the newly cut envelope together so that the tissue paper is on the inside. Glue the flaps down with white glue. To avoid messy globs, use a scrap of cardboard to squeegee off any excess glue before folding the flaps over.

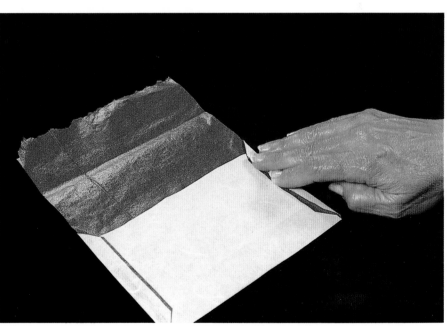

Chapter Five

PAPERMAKING

As environmental consciousness grows, the art of papermaking has become more and more popular. Wastepaper can easily be recycled and transformed into beautiful, sophisticated gift sets and even three-dimensional cast objects.

Moreover, tastes have changed. The slick, glossy, polished look of the 1980s has been replaced by a more muted, natural aesthetic. Handmade paper creations are very popular these days and always receive rave reviews.

I keep a small, clean wastebasket for papers I would ordinarily throw out and save as much as possible. I also save scraps of gold and silver leaf, flower petals, pieces of grass, leaves and tiny bits of fabric. These can all be added to the papermaking mixture (called slurry) for highlight effects in the finished sheets. Once you've made several sheets of your own paper, you can then use them to create a potpourri of items, including cards, bookmarks, gift tags, gift sacks and even envelopes.

To make paper, you'll need to buy or make a two-part wooden frame (called a deckle and screen). You'll also need to have a blender and lots of space. Each piece of paper you make will need to be dried flat by itself. This project can be messy and time-consuming, so be sure to wear old clothes and schedule the activity on a day when you have a fair amount of free time.

*Handmade paper creations are very popular as both mascu-
line and feminine gifts. From this batch of paper, I was able
to create gift bags, note cards and envelopes. Papermaking
can be intriguing—no two batches ever turn out the same.*

How to Make Paper From Scratch

1 Fill one-third of a blender with water. Tear your scrap paper into "bite-size" pieces (1 inch or smaller) and add two or three generous handfuls to the blender.

2 Also add a piece of cotton linter, roughly 2 inches square, torn into pieces. Cotton linter can be purchased at any local art and craft store. It is a long-fibered paper that will add strength to your paper pulp. Turn the blender on high and whirl for two or three minutes.

3 Pour the blender mixture into a tub of water. The new mixture (now called slurry) should be 90 percent water and 10 percent paper pulp. It will probably take three blenders full of pulp to achieve this ratio. The more you increase your pulp percentage, the heavier your finished paper will be.

4 To spice up your paper, add scraps of gold leaf, flower petals, leaves, herbs—even bits of fruits and vegetables.

5 Swirl the slurry gently with your hands to mix the materials.

6 Place your wooden frame (called a deckle) on top of the screen, with the screen side up.

7 Holding the two pieces of the frame together, push it down into the slurry away from you.

8 Level the frame, then lift. Hold the two pieces together firmly and shake out the excess water.

9 Set the frame down on newspaper and lift off the deckle.

10 Place a piece of sheeting or paper towel over the frame, covering the newly cast piece of paper.

11 Flip the frame over onto newspaper so that the back of the frame is face up and the paper towel is on the bottom. Sponge the back of the screen repeatedly (at least three or four times) to remove excess water. The more water you sponge out, the faster the paper will dry.

12 Lift the frame off and allow the paper to dry on the paper towel.

To make a handmade paper card, simply fold a piece of handmade paper in half, then line the inside with a smoother toothed paper (such as regular writing paper or rice paper). Cut the lining paper slightly smaller than the outer shell of the card. Spray the back with acrylic spray mount and attach it to the inside of the shell.

To make the envelope:

1 Begin with two sheets of paper the same size. Hold one piece horizontally and fold the top over about 1 inch. This will become the flap of the envelope. Match up the second piece of paper with the first and tear about an inch off the top (so that it fits under the flap). Holding the two pieces together, punch holes around the edges. Also, punch a few holes along the top of the shorter piece of paper. Punch one hole in the folded flap of the longer piece of paper.

2 Thread paper raffia through the holes to hold the pieces together. Knot the ends of the raffia to hold in place. Embellish with a twig or feather for a natural look.

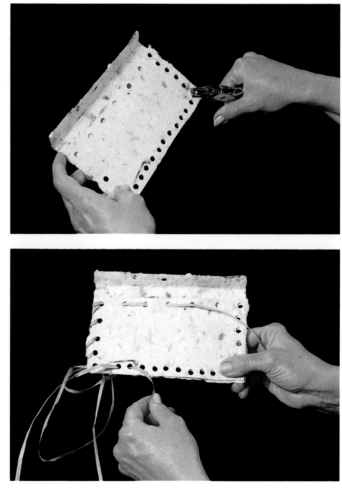

To make the gift bag:

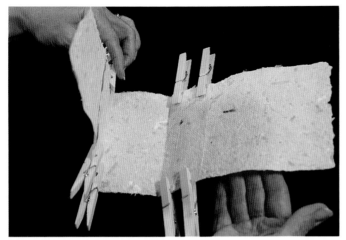

1 You'll need five sheets of hand-cast paper, all the same size. Begin by folding one piece of paper into thirds, vertically. This will create the bottom of your bag. Next, glue additional sheets of paper to the top third and bottom third of the folded paper. These will serve as the front and back of the bag. Secure the pieces with clothespins until the glue has dried.

2 To make the sides, fold two pieces of paper into accordion pleats lengthwise.

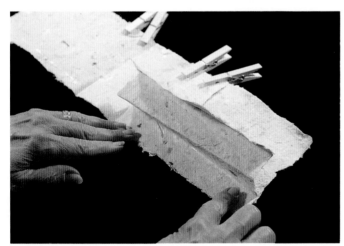

3 Glue one end of the accordion pleat to the inside of the front of the bag.

4 Stand the bag on end. Glue the other side of the accordion pleat to the inside of the back of the bag. Secure in place with clothespins until the glue is dry. Repeat the process on the other side of the bag.

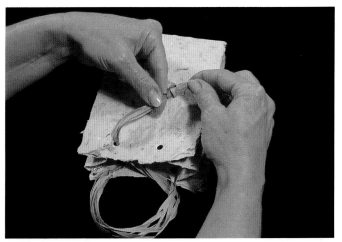

5 Once the bag is dry, punch four holes—two on the front panel and two on the back panel—to insert a handle.

6 Thread brown paper raffia (or the ribbon of your choice) through the holes to create a handle.

The finished bag can be used for a multitude of purposes, including birthday gifts and party favors.

Casting

Almost any mold that is concave can be used to create relief paper sculptures. Handmade paper will take on the shape of the mold if the paper is pressed in while still wet. Generally, it's best to use a simple mold without complex grooves—especially if your slurry is particularly thick and chunky.

For the keepsake card shown below, I used only pure white paper scraps in the slurry. I wanted the finished piece to have the bleached look of a time-worn, wave-battered seashell.

Before beginning this project, be sure to read the instructions for papermaking on pages 82-84.

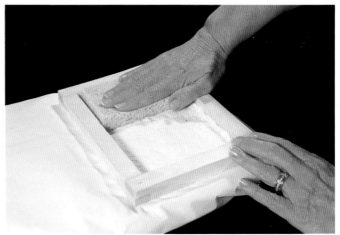

1 Culinary molds work well for paper casting. I found these synthetic scallop shells in a gourmet cooking shop and decided to give them a try.

3 Blend on high for 2 to 3 minutes. Then, over a sink, pour the slurry directly into the screen part of your frame (you need not use the deckle). Transfer the frame to a paper towel and sponge out the excess water.

2 The slurry you mix for molding purposes should be heavier than normal slurry used in paper-making. For this project I used scraps of heavy water-color paper. I also added extra cotton linter to the mix for strength (a 4″ × 4″ sheet did the trick).

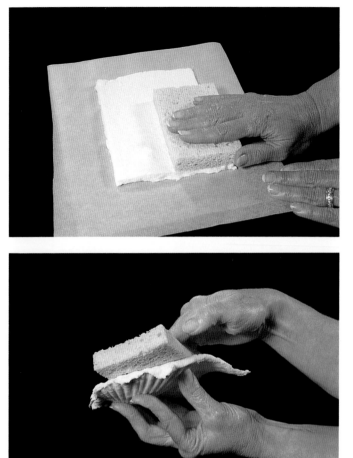

4 Remove the frame and continue sponging to remove more water. The paper should be nearly ⅛-inch thick.

5 Before you begin casting, wax your mold or grease it with a light coat of petroleum jelly. This will keep the paper from sticking to the mold when it dries. Press the paper into the mold with the sponge, carefully working it into all the curves and grooves. Allow several days of drying time.

6 Once the paper is completely dry, remove the cast from the mold. Glue the shell onto a heavy paper or card stock with strong white glue.

Cast paper molds can also be purchased ready-made from craft shops. I embellished this 3-D heart design with pastel watercolor washes, pearls and jewels to create a feminine, all-occasion card.

This charming cast paper house (purchased ready-made) made an adorable holiday card once livened up with a few touches of acrylic.

Chapter Six

EMBOSSING

Embossing can be time-consuming, but often adds just the right touch of elegance to very special cards and gifts. The technique involves raising the surface of the paper by pressing on the underside of the paper with a blunt tool. The result is a subtle, highly sophisticated look that works perfectly for bridal shower, wedding and formal dinner party invitations, thank-you cards and more.

To achieve a clean finish, it's always best to use a stencil design and a medium-weight paper, such as watercolor paper or card stock. Thin paper won't hold an impression and may tear. Paper that is too thick will be difficult to press into. Any small stencil can be used. You can even design and cut your own stencils if you wish. Many craft suppliers sell sheets of vellum or plastic specifically designed for embossing.

For professional results, you can buy an embossing tool or use some other object, such as the end of a small crochet hook or a blunt darning needle.

I like to use a light table for embossing so I can easily see which areas have been covered. I purchased a small child's light table from a toy store, and it works beautifully. If you don't own a light table, you can create one by working on a piece of glass and shining a lamp or flashlight underneath it. It also helps to spray paint your stencil a different color than the paper surface you're working with so it's easier to see.

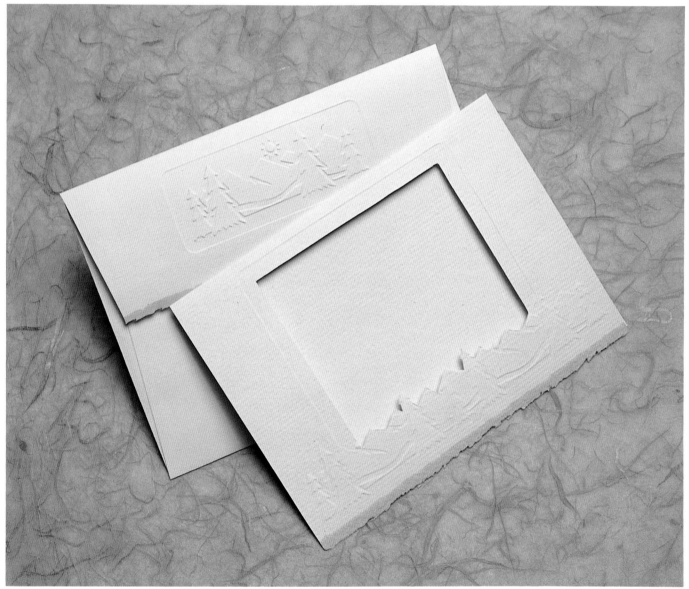

Because embossing can be time-consuming, it's best to use it to dress up small areas, such as borders. To create this adorable card, I first embossed the mountain scene onto medium-weight paper. Next, I cut out the window, carefully working around the mountains in the bottom of the window.

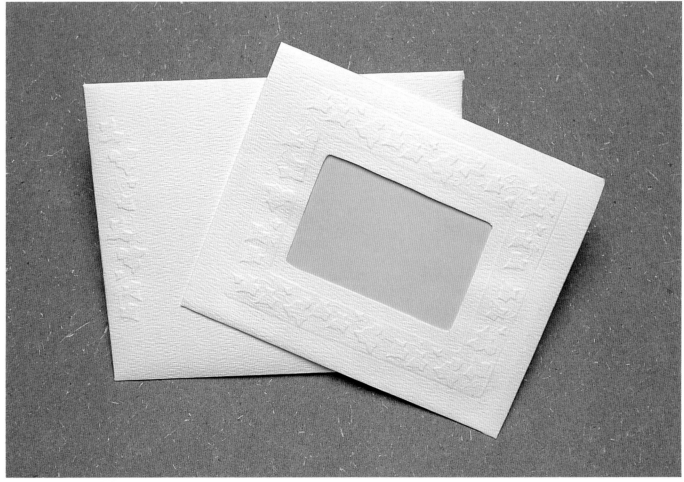

The window in this ivy-bordered card provides a perfect inset for a photo, phrase or pressed flower arrangement.

1 Begin by penciling in some guidelines for your border on the underside of the front of the card. (Remember that you'll be pressing on the underside of the paper to achieve the raised effect.)

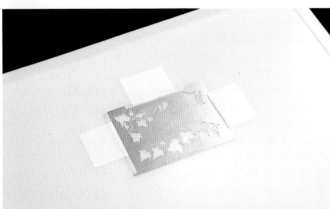

2 Tape your stencil to the light box or surface you'll be working on. This will prevent it from moving while you're embossing.

3 Position your card over the stencil so that the stencil design is directly under the area you wish to emboss. Be sure to place the card face down.

4 Press firmly inside the stencil holes with the embossing tool to make an impression in the paper.

5 Cut out the window in the center with a utility knife.

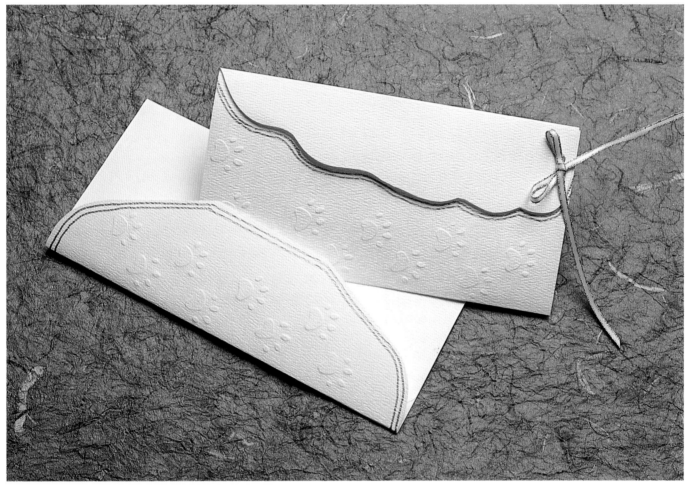

Paw prints on a scallop-edged card and matching envelope
are charming for a perfect, all-occasion gift.

Chapter Seven

METALLIC LEAFING

Metallic leaf can be applied to almost any clean, well-sealed surface and adds a touch of class to any card or gift. Like embossing, the technique can be time-consuming, so it is best used in small areas. Metallic leafing lends itself well to items such as table place cards, gift enclosures and borders.

Traditionally, an oxide red base coat was always used under gold leaf to enhance the color of the gold with time. When the leaf cracked, the red would show through. Today, you can find almost any color underneath gold leaf. Metallic leaf also comes in silver, copper, bronze and variegated colors.

I seldom use real gold leaf, as the cost is prohibitive. Imitation gold leaf, however, comes in little booklets and can be purchased for under ten dollars. Imitation leaf is actually a metal alloy, but it is so attractive that even the most skilled eye can have difficulty determining whether it is real or not. Provided it is sealed properly, imitation leaf will not tarnish.

Because metallic leaf is extremely fragile, you'll need to purchase a special adhesive called "sizing." It's best to work with very small amounts of leafing at a time. Take your time and apply it in patches. If you do try to handle large portions all at once you may accidentally bunch or tear the leaf, rendering it unusable.

Any type of sealed cardboard or paper can be leafed. I adorned this charming gift tie-on with a pine cone for a natural look.

For this project, we gathered some lovely leaves that had
fallen from the trees, and for a very special golden wedding
anniversary, we gilded the leaves to make place cards.

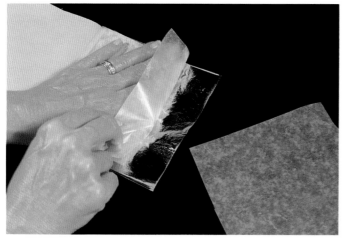

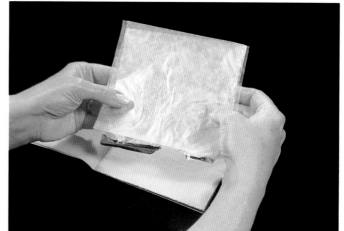

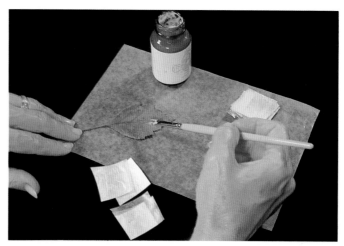

1 Select a few dried leaves (or other objects you wish to use) and seal them with several light coats of clear acrylic spray. To pick up a piece of gold leaf, place a small piece of wax paper on top of it and lay your hand flat on top of the wax paper. (The leaf cannot be picked up directly—it will tear.) The heat from your hand will cause the leaf to adhere to the wax paper.

2 Pick up the gold leaf and place another piece of wax paper on the other side, forming a sandwich. This will enable you to cut the gold leaf to the desired size without tearing it.

3 If possible, cut the gold leaf in proportion to the object you are leafing. If the object you are covering is very large, use several sheets of leaf and cover it in patches. Don't try to use a whole sheet of gold leaf all at once. It's easier to manage in small pieces.

4 With a small brush, apply the glue sizing to the surface you are leafing. At first, the glue will appear white. Once it turns clear, you can apply the gold leaf.

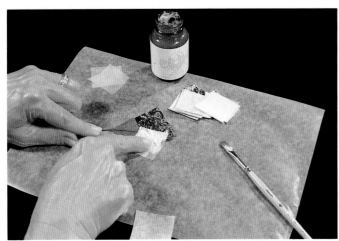

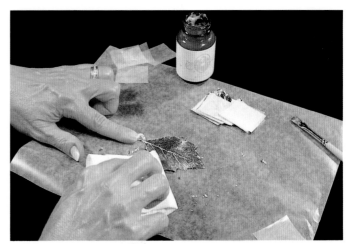

5 Remove one side of the wax paper sandwich and apply the exposed leaf to your surface. (It doesn't matter which side of the gold leaf you use. There is no front or back.) Continue to apply sheets of gold leaf until your object is covered. Don't worry if the sheets overlap. The gold will adhere only where it touches sizing. Once your object is completely covered, take a sheet of wax paper and pat the leafing down firmly to ensure it is completely adhered. Then, set it aside overnight.

6 The next day, remove the wax paper and burnish the surface of the object with a soft cloth such as chamois or velveteen. Rub the surface in one direction only. If any of the gold leaf comes off, simply add a touch of sizing and apply scraps of gold to the empty spots. When you've finished, seal the object again with a few light coats of acrylic spray fixative. This will keep it from tarnishing.

7 Glue the leafed object to your card with white glue. To echo the gold leaf on these place cards, I used a gold metallic liner pen to write in the names of the guests on the cards.

To create this gilded card, I painted sizing on the grape design and the card border, then applied gold leaf. The leaf adhered only to the areas painted with sizing. For depth and dimension, I rounded the grapes with a touch of burnt umber oil paint. To finish, I added curlicues with a gold metallic marking pen.

Chapter Eight

QUILLING

As early as 1700, beautiful filigree work, known today as "quilling," was collected and respected by English royalty. In 1791, Charles Elliott, a royal tradesman, supplied Princess Elizabeth with different filigree papers, one ounce of gold, and a box with ebony moldings, made for filigree work.

In this meticulous craft, strips of paper—often colored or gilt-edged—are rolled into circles, cones or spirals, then pinched into shapes. Each shape is then glued on one edge to a background of paper, silk or wood. The dainty, fragile scrolls resemble intricate metal filigree.

Special quilling paper and tools are available in many art and craft stores. The paper comes in a marvelous palette of at least fifty different colors, and is relatively inexpensive.

To create scrolled shapes, quilling paper is tightly rolled around a quilling tool (resembling a tiny knitting needle). Quilling tools come in two varieties: straight and slotted. A straight tool produces the tightest scrolls, but can sometimes be difficult to master. The slotted tool makes it easy to start rolling by providing a catch for the end of the paper. However, the slotted tool often leaves a messy creased area in the center of the scroll.

Quilling can be painstaking work and requires lots of practice, but the results are well worth the effort. It is a delicate and feminine-looking art form.

This delicately quilled card made a perfect keepsake for a new baby. Plus, it drew a huge smile from the new, proud parents.

Buttercups

This simple, elegant buttercup card was created by pinching a few simple scrolls into hearts and almond shapes.

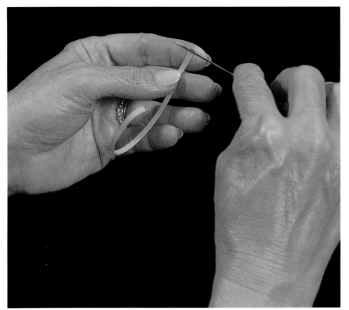

1 Cut a 6-inch length of quilling paper (the color of your choice). Moisten the end of the paper and begin wrapping it tightly around the end of the quilling tool. Moistening the end will help to hold it in place. Do not twist the tool. Wrap the paper tightly and carefully.

2 Continue to wrap the paper over top of itself as tightly as possible until you reach the end.

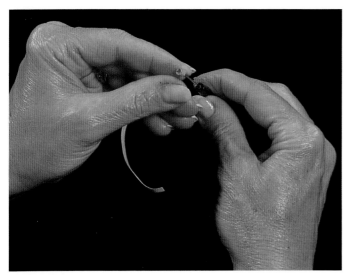

3 When you reach the end, apply a touch of white glue with a stylus and glue the end down to create a tight scroll. Remove the scroll from the tool.

4 Create a heart shape by pinching one side of the circle into a point. Then push in the opposite side with your fingernail. The heart shape will serve as one petal. Complete the entire process until you have created three petals. To create a leaf, roll a scroll with green paper. Pinch the scroll on two sides to make an almond shape.

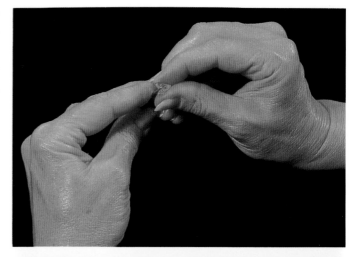

5 To assemble your flower, place the petals on a sheet of wax paper and attach them together, using a stylus to apply tiny bits of white glue. Add a stem of green paper and the green leaves you've created. You may want to hold the pieces in place with straight pins while they are drying.

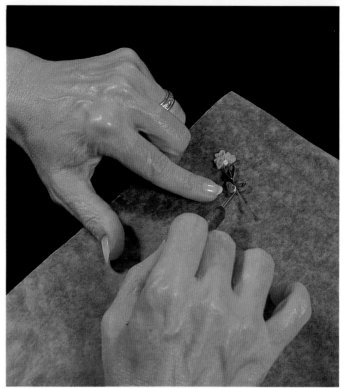

6 Once dry, transfer the flower to your card surface and glue in place with tacky glue.

Mushrooms

Tiny mushroom caps are easily created by pushing out the centers of paper scrolls. They can then be used to create darling gift tags or place cards.

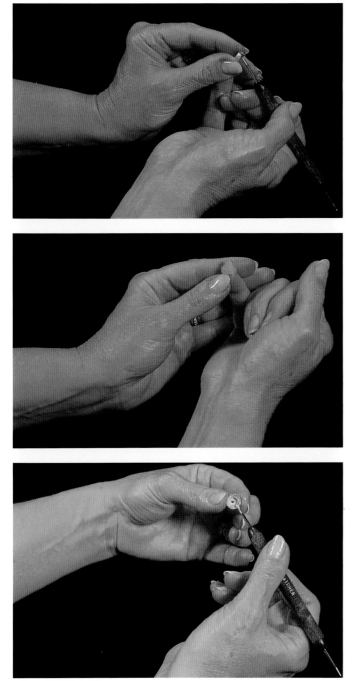

1 To create a mushroom cap, roll a tight scroll to the size you desire. The longer your paper, the larger the mushroom cap will be. Glue the end of the scroll and allow it to dry.

2 Using a stylus or the tip of your fingernail, push the center of the scroll outward to form a little crown.

3 Apply some white glue to the inside of the cap with a stylus or toothpick. The glue will keep the shape from collapsing. Allow this to dry.

I added a green stem with a loosely scrolled leaf to this mushroom cap. The result is a darling place card. I was careful to leave room to write in the name of a guest.

Dandelion Flowers

A combination of tiny fringed flowers (like dandelions) and scrolls makes a gorgeous keepsake birthday greeting.

1 To create a flower with fringed petals, simply cut a fringed pattern in the quilling paper before you begin rolling. The more space you leave between cuts, the larger your flower petals will be. It's best to use sewing or manicure scissors with small blades. Take care not to cut all the way through the paper as you are fringing it. You can also buy a special fringing tool at some craft stores.

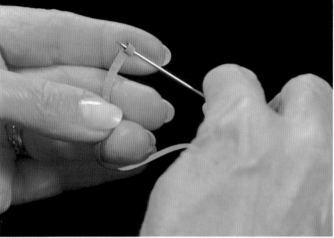

2 Roll the fringed paper around your quilling tool as tightly as possible and glue the end. Remove the tool.

3 Once dry, set the scroll fringe side up and primp the fringes into bloom with a stylus. The resulting flower will resemble a dandelion, marigold or carnation.

Index

Create Wonderful Crafts with these Great Books!

The Complete Book of Greeting Card Design & Illustration — Former art director of Hallmark Cards, Eva Szela, shows you a shop's worth of good wishes, congratulations, giggles and grins — all sure to sell! *#30573/$29.95/144 pages*

How to Write & Sell Greeting Cards, Bumper Stickers, T-Shirts, and Other Fun Stuff — Break into this lucrative market with valuable advice on how to create and sell "can't miss" novelty items.
#10280/$15.95/176 pages/paperback

Stencil Sourcebook — Transform drab furniture and ho-hum rooms into beautiful works of art! Here you'll get over 180 original designs you can turn into your own unique stencils.
#30595/$22.95/144 pages

Paper Craft — You'll be proud to display the charming and imaginative crafts you make with easy-to-follow instructions and illustrations.
#30530/$14.95/144 pages/paperback

Nature Craft — Detailed instructions and photographs make it easy to capture the wonder of outdoors in beautiful and unique crafts!
#30531/$14.95/144 pages/paperback

The Craft Supply Sourcebook — Let this easy shop-by-mail guide make it easy to find the materials you need for all your crafts — without ever leaving home!
#70144/$16.95/288 pages/paperback

The Complete Flower Arranging Book — You'll discover how to create more than 100 of the newest and most exquisite arrangements with fresh and dried flowers.
#30405/$24.95/192 pages

The Complete Flower Craft Book — Discover how to create a veritable bouquet of beautiful crafts! Packed with photographs and tips, each project will give you a garden of ideas and inspiration!
#30589/$24.95/144 pages

Great Gifts You Can Make in Minutes — You'll find the perfect gift for any occasion! In-depth instructions show you how to make more than 200 gifts — all for under $25!
#30427/$15.95/128 pages/paperback

Master Strokes — You'll master the techniques of using decorative paint finishes on everything from furniture, to walls, to floors with the helpful hints in this fully illustrated guide.
#30347/$27.95/160 pages/paperback

Creative Paint Finishes for the Home — Dozens of demonstrations show you how to beautify furniture, walls, and more with unique decorative paint finishes.
#30426/$27.95/144 pages

The Complete Book of Silk Painting — From setting up a workspace to selecting the best materials — you'll learn everything you need to know about the beautiful art of silk painting.
#30362/$24.95/128 pages

The Christmas Lover's Handbook — From gift wrapping to hundreds of handcrafted gift ideas, find everything you need to create a fabulous Christmas season. *#70221/$14.95/256 pages/paperback*

Make Your Own Picture Frames — You'll construct lovely and lasting frames with expert instruction on matting, assembling, finishing, hanging and more!
#30065/$12.95/144 pages/paperback

Creative Basketmaking — Create wonderfully unique, colorful and useful baskets with the step-by-step instructions in this easy-to-use guide.
#30164/$24.95/160 pages

Painting Murals — Learn how to beautify your home with this unique art! From choosing a subject to preparing the final surface, this step-by-step guide leads you every step of the way.
#30081/$27.95/168 pages

8548